Miles of Smiles

by Laurie Calkhoven
illustrations by Shannon Laskey

★ American Girl®

Questions or comments? Call 1-800-845-0005,
visit our Web site at **americangirl.com**,
or write to Customer Service, American Girl,
8400 Fairway Place, Middleton, WI 53562-0497.

Printed in China

10 11 12 13 14 15 LEO 13 12 11 10 9 8 7

All American Girl marks are trademarks of American Girl, LLC.

Editorial Development: Sara Hunt

Art Direction and Design: Camela Decaire

Production: Mindy Rappe, Kendra Schluter, Jeannette Bailey, Judith Lary

Illustrations: Shannon Laskey

Dear Traveler,

As you take to the road on your next adventure, pack this book for miles of smiles along the way. Start with **10 tips for travel.** Turn the pages to take **quizzes that clue you in** to your personal travel style, tell you whether you're open to adventure, and help you decide what type of theme park is best for you. Then flip to the **puzzle section** for cross grids, word searches, and brain benders with a travel twist.

Tucked into the back of the book is a **travel journal** just for you, a **board game** to play when you're bored, and a set of two-sided **game cards** with 24 ideas for something to do while you're on the road. You may never have to ask the question *"Are we there yet?"* again!

Happy travels.

Your friends at American Girl

Contents

Quizzes

AIRPORT

Puzzles

Inserts:

Travel Journal

Game Cards

Bored Game

TOP 10
Travel Tips

Follow these tips to have the most fabulous vacation ever!

Planning Ahead

10. Make a list of everything you'll need before hitting the road. Then check off items as you pack. When you're through, pack your packing list! This way you'll know what you brought, and you can make sure everything makes its way back home again when you repack after your visit.

9. Fill a backpack with boredom busters—like this book, colored pencils, markers, postcard stamps, your address book, and anything else you'll need to keep yourself busy. Be sure to leave some space to fill with souvenirs to take home.

8. Check your camera a few days before you leave. Do you have enough film? Is your battery charged? Do you need to stop by the store for a disposable camera? If so, add that to your packing list.

Staying Healthy

7. Feeling queasy in the backseat or on takeoff and landing? Simply closing your eyes can really help fight nausea. Eating saltine crackers can also help settle your stomach. Get some fresh air by rolling down a window in the car. On a plane, turn on your overhead vent. And don't be embarrassed to ask the flight attendant for an airsickness bag, just in case the worst happens.

6. It's easy to catch a cold in recirculated airplane air or when you're on the go. Wash your hands a lot, drink plenty of water, and try to get a good night's sleep every night while traveling.

5. Sunscreen isn't just for the beach. Whenever you will be outside, remember to slather it on 10 to 30 minutes before going outdoors.

More Good Advice for Girls on the Go

4. See you later, elevator! While it might be tempting to ride up and down on elevators just for the fun of it, it's actually not such a good idea because it disturbs other people who are trying to enjoy their vacation—and you could get hurt. Ditto for riding up and down escalators.

3. No more monkeys jumping on the beds! Jumping on the beds in hotel rooms might have been cute when you were littler, but now that you're old enough to know better, well . . . you're old enough to know better!

2. In public places, it's a good idea to make sure that you're always within eyesight of your grown-ups. How can you tell? If you can't see them, they can't see you! Plan with your group where to meet if you get separated. If you do get lost, report to the information booth or talk to someone in uniform who works at the park or hotel that you're lost in. That person can help you locate your missing grown-ups!

TOP TRAVEL TIP

1. Pack your patience and a smile!

Quizzes

What Kind of Traveler Are You?

Your bags are packed. You're ready to go—but where?
Answer the questions below to discover your travel style.
Circle the letter next to the answer that describes you best.

1. The Bath Shoppe just got in a new line of lotions. Which one would you choose?

a. Evergreen
b. Sparkle 'n' Shine
c. Cotton Candy
d. Vanilla Bean

2. You've been hearing about a new mall for weeks. You and your mom finally have a free afternoon to check it out. Where would you go first?

a. There's a rock-climbing wall! Need I say more?
b. window-shopping and people-watching
c. the directory at the information booth so that we can plan our route
d. the cinnamon-bun stand at the food court—mmm

3. Which one of these magazine headlines catches your eye at the newsstand?

a. "Riding the Roaring Rapids" in *Family Adventure Travel*
b. "Broadway's Biggest, Best Musicals" in *Big City Escapes*
c. "Top Ten Places to Visit" in *American Tourist*
d. "Create a Cool Bedroom Hideaway" in *Teen Decor*

11

4. Celebrities are coming to your local civic center for an autograph party. Who would you wait in line to meet?

a. X-treme snowboarder Buzzy Board
b. child musical phenom Veronica Violin
c. roller-coaster designer Rocky Ride
d. mystery writer Chloe Clue

5. Over spring break, your teacher said you could earn extra credit by doing one of these assignments. Which one would you pick?

a. Look for unusual plant species in your area.
b. Visit the local art museum and draw a picture of your favorite painting or sculpture.
c. Collect postcards while visiting the historical sites in your area.
d. Read about another country and give an oral report.

6. You've got your own personal time-travel machine! Where would you go?

a. I'd travel to the future and be on the first charter flight to the moon.
b. I'd see the Statue of Liberty arrive in New York City.
c. I'd go to the opening ceremony of the Olympics —the 2030 Olympics, that is.
d. I'd go back in time and dance at my grandparents' wedding.

Gate E
Gate D

7. You've just heard that you're going to spend a week at a ski lodge. What are you looking forward to most?

a. racing down the slopes
b. meeting new people from places I've never been
c. that great view of everything from the chair lift
d. sipping hot chocolate by the fire in the lodge

8. If you were an ice-cream flavor, which one would you be?

a. Rocky Road (a little nutty and very sweet)
b. Parisian Vanilla (not just plain vanilla—stylish and sophisticated)
c. Bubble Gum (pop-ular, like a party in your mouth)
d. Cookie Dough (sweet and smooth, with just the right touch of homey goodness)

9. Which one of these collections would most likely be found in your room?

a. pictures of me at the top of a trail, at the bottom of a slope, and on the crest of a wave
b. snow globes with scenes from around the world
c. T-shirts from all the great places I've visited
d. postcards from my friends

10. Your parents just brought home a stack of travel brochures. If you could, which one of these adventures would you choose?

a. a trip through the Alaskan wilderness
b. an eight-city European tour
c. a week at the biggest, coolest theme park ever
d. a beach house with room for all my family and friends

11. It's your first day at a new summer camp. What's the first thing you do?

a. Get a trail map and plan a day hike.
b. Check out the arts and crafts cabin.
c. Grab an activity schedule and start planning—I don't want to miss the highlights.
d. Unpack my pillow and favorite stuffed animal so that I feel at home.

Answers

Mostly a's
Bold and Intrepid
When it comes to traveling, you're always ready to take on new challenges and adventures. You love to be outdoors and on the move, whether you're learning a new sport, hiking a killer trail, or racing down a mountain.

Mostly b's
City Sophisticate
Nature can be beautiful, but at heart you're a city girl. City Sophisticates like you want to be in the center of the action. Art, music, and other cultural happenings make the big city the place to be! You love to learn new things and meet new people on your big-city travel adventures.

Mostly c's
Tourist Trekker

You might not want to go on a three-mile hike or spend all your time in the arts and crafts cabin, but you don't want to miss any of the highlights either. You're a Tourist Trekker, a traveler who likes to hit all the major hot spots, even if you have time for only a quick peek and a trip to the souvenir shop.

Mostly d's
Armchair Traveler

You're so happy at home that travel isn't high on your list of things to do. Reading about interesting places can be almost as exciting as going there, but everyone has to leave home sometimes. When you do travel, just be sure to bring some of your favorite things—like your pillow and a favorite stuffed animal—to make your stay comfy and cozy.

Planes, Trains, and Automobiles

Answer the questions below and find the mode of transportation that's best for you. When you're done, quiz your travel partners, too!

1. When your alarm clock goes off in the morning, you . . .

a. jump out of bed, ready to start a new day.
b. roll over and start thinking about your plans for the day.
c. pull the blanket over your head and snuggle under the covers for as long as you can.

2. Which one of these animals would you say is most like you?

a. an eagle
b. a horse
c. a turtle

3. You're traveling and you're hungry. What would you prefer for eats along the way?

a. an extra bag of pretzels (then go out to eat when we get there)
b. a concession stand with a simple menu of choices
c. a food court, with lots and lots of fast options

4. Your favorite aunt has to miss your party, but her present arrives two days before your birthday. When will you open it?

    a. the second the mailman leaves—I'm too excited to wait
    b. first thing on the morning of my birthday
    c. at my party, after birthday games and cake

5. Sign up for one of these field-day activities.

    a. 50-yard dash
    b. three-legged race
    c. carrying an egg on a spoon

6. You're late to meet your friends at the July 4th picnic, and the neighborhood park is a twenty-minute walk away. You . . .

    a. ride your bike as fast as you can. You'll cool off when you get there.
    b. in-line skate so that you're not too late or too overheated.
    c. definitely walk. It's too hot to run. Besides, that birdhouse along the way is so cool—you've got to see it!

7. When you're traveling, your family likes to . . .

a. get where you're going as fast as possible.
b. sit back and enjoy the scenery—what's the big rush?
c. take spontaneous detours to places like Lizard Village and Big Bob's Banana Boat Museum.

8. If you're sitting next to your sister or a friend on a trip, you're more likely to . . .

a. shout, "She touched my seat."
b. play together for a while, then do your own thing.
c. play games and braid each other's hair.

9. It's late at night as you're heading to your destination. You close your eyes and . . .

a. think of all the exciting things that you'll do on vacation—you can't wait!
b. nod off, but then wake up again every time you feel a bump.
c. fall asleep—you can catch zzz's just about anywhere!

10. At the carnival, your favorite thing to do is . . .

a. conquer the tallest, fastest ride. Who cares if there's a line!
b. ride the trolley around the whole carnival to see everything there is before picking what to do first.
c. zip around in the bumper cars; you like to be safely on the ground.

Answers

Mostly a's
Plane

You're in a hurry to get where you're going and you like to go fast! Fasten your seat belt and put your tray table in the upright position for your airplane ride. Don't forget to slow down enough to enjoy the view if you're lucky enough to get the window seat.

Mostly b's
Train

You want to get where you're going, but you're not in such a big hurry that you'll give up personal comfort to get there. You and your family might consider train travel as an option for an upcoming trip.

Mostly c's
Automobile

Planning your vacation is just as much fun for you as the vacation itself. You like to set your own schedule and take spur-of-the-moment detours. Fill up the gas tank and pack the trunk—traveling by car is the perfect plan for you.

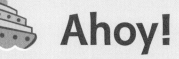

Ahoy!

Climb aboard the cruise ship *SS American Girl* and sail away. Answer the questions below to find the role that suits you best on the friendly seas.

1. You've got a big science test in a week. Which of the following describes your study style?

    a. I invite my friends over for a study group so that we can quiz one another.
    b. I organize my notes into species and subspecies and study one per day.
    c. I paid attention in class, so all I need to do is review my notes on the bus that morning.
    d. I agree to join my friend's study group.

2. At the end-of-camp bonfire party, which best-camper award would you win?

    a. most social
    b. neatest bunk
    c. biggest daredevil
    d. happiest camper

3. Which one of these birthday parties would you plan for yourself?

    a. a board-game extravaganza at home
    b. an afternoon movie followed by reservations at my fave pizza parlor
    c. horseback riding at the local stables
    d. nothing fancy, just a sleepover with all my friends

4. Which one of these after-school clubs would you join?

a. Pep Squad
b. Computer Club
c. Gymnastics Club
d. Reading Brigade

5. Which one of these phrases best describes you?

a. friendly and easygoing
b. smart and organized
c. brave and spontaneous
d. laid-back and happy

6. Your family's spending a week at the beach! When you're not building sand castles, you're . . .

a. organizing a family mini-golf tournament.
b. checking out brochures for nearby tourist attractions.
c. taking surfing lessons.
d. swimming and jumping in the waves.

7. Your class is dividing into teams for a scavenger hunt. You . . .

a. help when you can and cheer on your team.
b. check off items on the list as your team finds them.
c. lead your team around the school as you crack the clues.
d. follow the leader and keep your eyes peeled.

8. For your school's annual talent show, you . . .

a. sign up students and teachers for the show.
b. sell tickets and seat guests.
c. form a band and lead them in a rocking version of the school song.
d. dance a hip-hop routine with your friends.

Answers

Mostly a's
Cruise Director

You're friendly and know how to cheer on a team. As Cruise Director on the *SS American Girl*, you'll organize games and activities to keep the passengers busy and happy.

Mostly b's
Travel Agent

You're organized and responsible—not to mention on top of every detail. As the Travel Agent for the *SS American Girl*, you'll book passengers on the vacation of their dreams.

Mostly c's
Ship's Captain
You're a leader and you're adventurous—the perfect combination to be the Captain of the *SS American Girl*. You have the courage and the smarts to keep the ship running smoothly.

Mostly d's
Happy Passenger
You're easygoing and love spending time with your friends. Sit back, relax, ask for a little umbrella in your lemonade, and enjoy your poolside snacks, because you're a Happy Passenger!

Ty Ultimate Theme-Park Mania

You have only a few days to spend—and so many things to do! How do you pick **which theme park to check out?** Take this quiz to learn where you'll have the best time.

1. Who or what would you most like to see?

a. monkeys
b. people from countries I've never been to
c. princesses
d. movie monsters

2. Your favorite amusement park ride is . . .

a. a water slide into a dolphin pool.
b. a rocket ship to Mars.
c. a carousel with handsome horses and a pumpkin coach.
d. a rock-and-roller coaster.

3. Which one of these reality shows would you most like to star in?

   a. *African Safari*
   b. *Destination Space*
   c. *Princess for a Day*
   d. *Broadway Star*

4. Which one of these vacations would you have the most fun on?

   a. a whale-watching cruise in Alaska
   b. a trip around the world
   c. a visit to ancient castles in Europe
   d. Hollywood!

5. What kinds of stories do you like best?

   a. animal adventures
   b. science-fiction stories
   c. fairy tales
   d. action adventures

6. Where would you like to spend a Saturday night?

   a. the zoo
   b. the planetarium
   c. a dance recital
   d. a movie premiere

7. Choose one of these Halloween costumes.

   a. a lion
   b. a mad scientist/inventor
   c. a ballerina
   d. an ogre

8. Which would you rather do?

   a. learn the secrets of a crocodile hunter
   b. go on a mock space flight with real astronauts
   c. have breakfast with princesses
   d. get my picture taken with my favorite movie star

Answers

Mostly a's
Safari and Ocean World
You love all kinds of creatures, whether they live on land or at sea. Safari and Ocean World is the perfect theme park for you. Go on a wild adventure across the African plains, swim with the dolphins, and explore the unpredictable natural world!

Mostly b's
World of Wonder
Check out World of Wonder, the place to learn about cultures from all over the world and find out what's coming in the future! On your awesome adventure, you'll travel through time and space in a park where reality is fantastic.

Mostly c's
Fantasy Fest

You love storybook princesses and their fantasy world, and that's just where you should go! Enchanted creatures come to life and every day is "Once upon a time . . ." Fantasy Fest is the theme park where all your dreams come true.

Mostly d's
Showbiz World

Step into the bright lights of show business and see how movie makers come up with those amazing special effects at Showbiz World—the perfect theme park for a girl who's ready to hit the big time. You'll find yourself in a front-row seat for an extravaganza!

Are You Open to Adventure?

How open to new experiences are you? Are you willing to **sample new foods, make new friends,** and **explore new interests?** Take this quiz to see where you fall on the fun-o-meter.

1. Your friend's family is hosting a Japanese exchange student and invites you to a special dinner in her honor. When you arrive, you discover that not only is the exchange student Japanese, but so is the food! You . . .

   a. taste the sushi. "Hey, it's pretty good!"
   b. say, "Uh, I'll just have some white rice, please."

2. The lakeside cabin your family stays in every summer isn't available this year. You say . . .

   a. "Great! I love the old cabin, but now we get to try something new."
   b. "Now our vacation is ruined!"

3. You and your best friend always go to a movie and then have a sleepover on the last day of school. This year, she wants to throw a backyard barbecue instead and invite your whole class. You . . .

   a. think a barbecue sounds like a lot of fun, and ask if some of your friends can stay for the sleepover.
   b. try to talk her out of it. Going to the movies is what you always do. Why change?

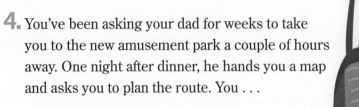

4. You've been asking your dad for weeks to take you to the new amusement park a couple of hours away. One night after dinner, he hands you a map and asks you to plan the route. You . . .

a. grab the map and get to work. Roller coasters, here you come!

b. say, "Hey, I don't drive. How am I supposed to figure this out?"

5. There's a girl your age staying in the room next door to yours at the ski lodge. You . . .

a. introduce yourself and ask her if she wants to join you on the slopes.

b. smile when you see her and hope she starts a conversation.

6. The new girl at school invited you to a horseback-riding party. The only problem? You've never been on a horse. You . . .

a. grab the reins and yell, "Giddyup."

b. make up an excuse not to go. You don't want to embarrass yourself by falling off.

7. It's time for your family's annual vacation-planning meeting, and your mom has an armful of brochures. You . . .

    a. look at all the cool places there are to visit and wonder how you'll ever choose.

    b. urge your siblings to vote for the same beach you went to last year. That was fun!

8. You're about to go on a seven-mile hike through the woods, and your camp counselor is explaining what to do if you get lost. But she says something that doesn't quite make sense. So you . . .

    a. raise your hand and ask her to explain.

    b. keep your mouth shut. You don't want to look stupid in front of the other kids.

BALLOON ADVENTURES

FUN-O-METER

Answers

Give yourself two points for every **a** answer and one point for every **b.**

14–16 points

Wow! You're open for fun. You take advantage of every new opportunity to have a good time, and you're not afraid to ask questions when you need to. You're friendly and adventurous and willing to try anything once. Do you sometimes jump in too fast? Ask for safety tips before you climb on that horse, and don't forget to wear a helmet.

11–13 points

You're getting there! You like to try new things and make new friends, but you can be too attached to the way things have always been. Sometimes it's smart to stand back before diving into a new experience, but don't let your shyness get in the way of having fun.

8–10 points

Uh-oh! When it comes to trying new things, meeting new people, and having new experiences, your answer is usually "No, thanks!" Next time, don't be so quick to say no to something new. Everyone gets shy and nervous in new situations. The trick is to try to relax and have fun.

Carry On

Look at the contents of each backpack below and select the one that looks most like yours on a long trip. Then turn the page and see what your pick says about you!

- a camera
- funny sunglasses with palm trees on them
- some chocolate sandwich cookies
- a puzzle/activity book
- a mix of pop and rock tunes
- a colorful scrunchie
- yarn balls—to learn how to juggle

- my hiking boots
- seashells and driftwood I collected
- oatmeal raisin cookies
- a nature guide
- country classics
- ponytail elastics
- hiking guide so that I can plan what trails to hit

- my journal
- a necklace I made out of shells and silk cord
- a giant frosted sugar cookie
- a sketch pad and colored pencils
- songs by an up-and-coming singer
- a headband that I decorated myself
- postcards to send to my friends

- Stuffy, my stuffed giraffe
- matching tie-dyed T-shirts for me and my mom
- homemade chocolate-chip cookies
- a novel about friendship
- Broadway show tunes
- butterfly barrettes I got for my last birthday
- backseat or airplane games for the whole family

- my CD or MP-3 player
- crazy board shorts
- gingersnaps
- a fantasy adventure novel
- new music I've never heard before that my friend recommended
- ribbons and beads for my braids
- a movie to watch on Mom's laptop

Answers

Mostly orange

You're strong, confident, and full of energy! You like your life to be exciting, and you love to try new things. Your friends love you for your hilarious sense of humor. Life with you is never boring.

Mostly green

You love the outdoors—camping, hiking, or just sitting under a tree with a book. You're easygoing and friendly, but you'd rather hang out with your family or a few best friends than go to a big party. Your friends love you for your calm self-confidence.

Mostly blue

You're artistic and creative. You can be shy at first, but once you get to know someone, you're the life of the party. You're a very loyal person. Your friends know they can count on you to be honest and true-blue.

Mostly pink

You put your family first. You're also the person your siblings and friends come running to when they need help or advice, and you're always happy to lend a hand. Sometimes you have to be reminded to take care of yourself—along with everyone else!

Mostly purple

You're a risk-taker! You're curious and funny and you love adventure—especially when you're the leader, not the follower. You also love to be the center of attention, and you're so much fun to be around that your friends don't mind.

Car Colors

Circle your favorite car. Then turn the page to see
how your car color "paints" your personality.

Answers

Red
You're bold and energetic. No goal is too large—whether it's getting an A in math or making the soccer team, you're always ready to tackle a challenge. But be careful! Red cars get more speeding tickets than any other color.

Blue
You're relaxed and peaceful. But that doesn't mean you're totally laid-back. You dream big, and you're persistent and creative when it comes to reaching your goals. You never give up!

Orange
You're hip and trendy. You always know all about the new bands or the hottest new celebs. But that doesn't mean you're shallow! Orange lovers are enthusiastic, happy, and always ready to do a good deed.

Silver
You're chic and sophisticated. Whether it's sushi at that new Japanese restaurant or the big new slide at the water park, you're the first to try new things. You're classy and original.

White

You're calm and organized. You're honest and you like to keep your things neat and clean. You're the first one your friends turn to when they need to borrow notes for a test or get a second opinion in the dressing room at the mall.

Green

You're easygoing, original, and love to relax and enjoy life—especially when you can be outdoors. But that doesn't mean you're not determined. You're always reaching for your dreams.

Yellow

You're active and optimistic. You love new adventures and are always ready to plan a road trip for you and your family. You're easygoing in groups but can always be counted on to get things done.

Black

You're a good leader—in charge and in control. But that doesn't mean you're stubborn. You're never afraid to stop and change tactics if things aren't working out the way you want them to.

My Dream Car

Travel Trivia!

Can you **stump the host** of this new game show, *Travel Trivia*? See if you can guess the answers to the weird and wacky questions below to win the grand prize.

1. The world's largest water park is in what state?

   a. Florida   b. Wisconsin

2. The state with the oldest baseball stadium:

   a. Illinois   b. Massachusetts

3. The country's longest interstate highway runs between these two cities:

   a. Boston and Seattle
   b. San Francisco and New York

4. Where can you ride the fastest roller coaster in the world?

   a. Ohio   b. New Jersey

5. Largest lake entirely in the U.S.:

   a. Lake Okeechobee, FL
   b. Lake Michigan

6. The southernmost point in the continental U.S. is:

a. Key West, FL   b. South Padre Island, TX

7. This state boasts the longest coastline:

a. Alaska   b. California

8. The busiest airport in the country is in what U.S. metropolitan area?

a. Atlanta   b. Dallas/Ft. Worth

9. Tallest Ferris wheel in North America:

a. Chicago's Navy Pier   b. Dallas's Fair Park

10. Largest shopping mall in the U.S.:

a. Mall of America, Minneapolis, MN
b. The Galleria, Houston, TX

ANSWERS

1. b.

Wisconsin is home to the water park "capital," Wisconsin Dells. Noah's Ark is the largest water park, and the Kalahari is the largest indoor water park.

2. b.

The Boston Red Sox won the World Series in 1912, the year that their stadium, Fenway Park, first opened. They didn't win another one in Fenway—the country's oldest baseball stadium—until 2004.

3. a.

The longest interstate highway in America is I-90, which runs from Boston to Seattle, a distance of 3,081 miles. I-80, which runs from San Francisco to Teaneck, New Jersey, is just 172 miles shorter than I-90.

4. b.

Kingda Ka at Six Flags Great Adventure in Jackson, New Jersey, reaches speeds of 128 miles per hour in three seconds. Coaster cars climb a 456-foot tower (that's more than 45 stories in the air!), then plummet 418 feet. *Whoosh!*

5. b.

America's largest lake is Lake Michigan, which borders the states of Illinois, Indiana, Michigan, and Wisconsin. Lake Michigan's surface area exceeds 22,000 square miles, while Lake Okeechobee covers less than 1,000 square miles in central Florida.

6. a.

The southernmost point in the continental United States is marked by a giant buoy in Key West, Florida. A sign on the face of this popular landmark reads "90 miles to Cuba."

7. a.

The state with the longest coastline is Alaska.

8. a.

Since 1998, Atlanta's Hartsfield-Jackson International Airport has been the world's busiest passenger airport.

9. b.

The Texas Star at Fair Park (Dallas) is home to the tallest Ferris wheel in North America at 212 feet (that's 64 feet taller than the Ferris wheel at Navy Pier). The Texas Star has a maximum capacity of 260 people.

10. a.

The Mall of America is the country's largest shopping mall—four stories tall with about 2.5 million square feet of retail space. Talk about shopping 'til you drop!

Airplane Explorer

The next time you soar through the clouds, **find out the answers** to these questions about your plane, your destination, and the people flying you there!

What kind of plane is it?

How many rows of seats are there?

How many seats are in your row?

Who are you sitting next to?

How many lavatories are on the plane?

Did your flight take off on time?

Is there an airsickness bag in your seat pocket?

Is there a magazine?

TRAY TABLES MUST BE I
POSITION FOR TAKEOFF

WELCOME TO AMERICAN GIRL AIRWAYS!

What else is in your seat pocket? ....

Where are you flying from? ....

What's your final destination? ....

Do you have a connecting flight? ....

How many bags did your family check? ....

How many bags did your family carry on? ....

How many flight attendants are there? ....

Ask one flight attendant his or her name, or read a name tag.

ES MUST BE IN THE UPRIGHT
OR TAKEOFF AND LANDING

FLIGHT
news
WELCOME

What's your cruising altitude? (The captain will announce it.)

Is there an in-flight movie?

Did the airline serve a snack, or did you bring your own?

Was there any turbulence, or was it a smooth flight?

Will your flight land on time, late, or ahead of schedule?

Did you say hello to the crew when you boarded?

Backseat Scavenger Hunt

How many of these items do you have in your car? Check them off to **explore how prepared you are** for your next family road trip.

Must-Haves

- ❏ Band-Aids
- ❏ Cell phone
- ❏ Computer printout of directions
- ❏ Driver's license
- ❏ First-aid kit
- ❏ Emergency road-service card
- ❏ Flashlight
- ❏ Garage door opener
- ❏ Insurance card
- ❏ Map
- ❏ Registration

Seasonal Basics

- ❏ Driving gloves
- ❏ Ice scraper
- ❏ Emergency water supply

Extras

- ❏ Baseball cap
- ❏ Snow boots
- ❏ Camera and film
- ❏ Change
- ❏ Crayons and drawing paper
- ❏ CD case and CDs
- ❏ Hairbrush or comb
- ❏ Parking pass
- ❏ Pen and paper
- ❏ Reading or puzzle book
- ❏ Snacks
- ❏ Sunscreen
- ❏ Sunglasses
- ❏ Tissues
- ❏ Trash bag

Scoring

Give yourself two points for every **Must-Have** or Seasonal Basic checked off your list and one point for every item on the Extras list.

0–15 points
Ready?

Your family car might not be ready to handle an emergency—or a bout of boredom—on the open road. Make sure you at least have the basics covered so that you can travel worry- and boredom-free!

16–35 points
Set

You've got the basics, but are you prepared for every road emergency? What if a brilliant thought crosses your mind, and you have nothing to write it down with? If you're going to be in the car for more than a few hours, add more items to your car.

36+ points
Go!

Not only is your family ready for every emergency, but you'll also have a blast on the way to wherever you're going. Pack your bags and plan your route—it's time for an awesome family road trip! But, hey, is it time to clean out the car? Maybe.

Whale-Watching 101

You forgot to bring your camera on the whale-watching voyage, but the view is so exciting that you're sure you'll remember it forever. Look at this page carefully. Then turn the page and see if you really have a photographic memory.

1. How many dolphins were there? ....

2. What was the captain holding? ....

3. What did it say on the back of the life jackets? ....

....

4. How many girls were wearing life jackets? ....

5. How many whales were in the water? ....

6. What did it say on the girl's tote bag? ....

Check the answers at the bottom of the page.

Scoring

1–2 correct	**3–4 correct**	**5–6 correct**
Out of Focus	Photogenic	Picture Perfect
Did you forget to use the flash? Make sure you have the correct "lighting" the next time, and you'll notice that the captain was holding a telescope, not a coffee cup.	Getting better, but you still missed some important details. Focus your "lens" on the scene before you, turn the page, and you'll be picture perfect in no time.	Wow, your mental "camera" is perfectly focused. You've got a photographic memory!

Answers: 1. three; 2. a telescope; 3. Whale of a Time Tours; 4. two; 5. three; 6. I "love" whales

Raccoon Tricks

How good are your powers of concentration? Try this **memory test.** A raccoon got curious about your family's tent while you were out on a hike. Now at least five things are missing. Can you tell what they are?

Look at this picture for one minute.

Time's up! Now do something else for a minute—check for new state license plates, hum a one-minute tune, or look out the airplane window to see what's below—anything you want. Make sure you wait at least a minute, and then turn the page.

List what's missing:

1. ....
2. ....
3. ....

4. ....
5. ....

Check the answers at the bottom of the page.

Scoring

1 or none right
Uh-oh!
You forgot to remember to concentrate. Try harder to focus when the details are super important.

2 or 3 right
Looking Good
You've got some of the details covered. When concentration is important, try to block out distractions and focus on the details.

4 or 5 right
Memory Ace!
You're all-powerful when it comes to memory and concentration! Your mind is razor sharp at noticing detail and remembering facts and figures.

Answers: tank top, log, flag, fish, ball, and, of course, the raccoon!

50

Postcards from the Road

Ready to tell your friends all about your crazy vacation? Fill in the blanks below with the first words that pop into your head. Don't read the sentences until you're done.

A **NOUN** is the name of a person, place, or thing. Car, airplane, book, arm, and sand are nouns.

A **VERB** is an action word. Drive, swim, scream, and throw are verbs.

An **ADJECTIVE** describes something or somebody. Pretty, blue, sparkly, and cold are adjectives.

An **EXCLAMATION** is a gasp or an outcry. Cool! Wow! and Ick! are exclamations.

Beach-Blanket Bingo

Dear _____ :
       (name)

We finally arrived at _____ . It was _____ . When we first
                        (body of water)   (adjective)

got here, we _____ a _____ and ate _____ . Dad yelled,
             (past-tense verb) (noun)   (noun)

" _____ !" We were surprised by the _____ who
   (exclamation)   (plural noun)

wanted to _____ in the water. It was _____ . After dinner we
           (verb)   (adjective)

went to the amusement park and rode the _____ . You should see
                                          (noun)

the _____ ! I rode the merry-go-round and _____ with
     (noun)   (past-tense verb)

a _____ .
   (noun)

See you soon!

Ski Bunnies on Parade

Dear _____ (name) :

We finally arrived at _____ (noun) . I couldn't wait to _____ (verb) , but I couldn't find my _____ (noun) . The lodge is so _____ (adjective) .

I ran into _____ (famous person) and we _____ (past-tense verb) . We started off with _____ (food) and _____ (food) , and then drank _____ (liquid) .

Tomorrow we're going to _____ (verb) . I'm taking lots of _____ (plural noun) with my camera. I bought you a _____ (noun) .

I hope it will _____ (verb) in my suitcase!

See you soon!

Roller Coaster Ride

Dear _____ (name) :

The _____ (last name) family ruled the theme park last week when Dad took me and _____ (boy's name) (my brother) on the _____ (adjective ending in "est") roller coaster we had ever seen—and we survived! Mom took one look at it and shook her _____ (noun) . "I'll wait here," she said. Dad, _____ (repeat boy's name) , and I got in line. "Are you sure?" Dad asked. "It's a _____ (noun) ." We were sure. We had to ride that _____ (noun) . I could hardly see the top, the coaster was so _____ (adjective) . I got on between _____ (repeat boy's name) and Dad, and then— _____ (exclamation) —we were off! It was super _____ (adjective) !

Wish you were here!

Puzzles

Vanity Tags

Can you **guess the meanings** of these vanity license plates?

NORTH CAROLINA
CRE8IV

1. ....

CALIFORNIA
ISK8

2. ....

VIRGINIA
IICPTN

3. ....

WISCONSIN
DOL LVR

4. ....

FLORIDA
LUV2SWM

5. ....

OHIO
PZA LVR

6. ....

ARIZONA
JUSBKZ

7. ....

UTAH
RDY2SKI

8. ....

CONNECTICUT
L84CLS

9. ....

TEXAS
HOWDEDU

10. ....

GEORGIA
10SNE1

11. ....

NEW HAMPSHIRE
SPR FAM

12. ....

NEW YORK
GDA M8

13. ....

KANSAS
AWSM TRP

14. ....

NEW MEXICO
IBCNU

15. ....

WASHINGTON
2N2R4

16. ....

VERMONT
ANML LVR

17. ....

Highway Puzzlers

Avoid a **traffic ticket** and guess what these highway signs mean.

1. ....

   ....

2. ....

   ....

3. ....

   ....

4. ....

   ....

5. ....

   ....

6. ....

   ....

7. ....

   ....

8. ....

9. ....

10. ....

11. ....

12. ....

13. ....

14. ....

Baggage Claim

You've claimed one of your suitcases, but its match is still on the baggage carousel. **Can you find it?**

Souvenirs for Sale

Emily and her brothers and sister each have $15.00 to spend at the theme park's souvenir shop. Use the grid below to fill in their purchases and find out who has $3.00 left to buy an ice cream cone.

Alexis, David, and Matt each buy five postcards for $1.00 to send to their friends, plus five 24-cent postcard stamps.

Emily buys a T-shirt with a picture of her favorite character for $12.50.

Alexis finds a cute lamp for her bedroom, and it's on sale for $12.00.

Emily and Matt both buy cool pens for $1.00 each.

David buys a rock-and-roller-coaster poster for his room for $5.00.

David borrows $1.00 from Matt to buy a DVD of the last night's musical and fireworks show for $8.00.

Alexis and Emily choose dolphin pins to attach to their backpacks for 50 cents each.

T-SHIRTS
$12.50

POSTCARDS
5 FOR $1

DOLPHIN PINS
50 CENTS

DVDS $8

POSTERS
$5.00

ICE CREAM
$3.00

LAMPS
$12.00

SOUVENIRS

Amount Spent

	Purchases	Purchases	Purchases	Money Left Over
David	2.20			
Emily				
Alexis	2.20			
Matt	2.20			

Making Friends All Over the World

How many ways can you say, "Hello. My name is . . ."?
Match the phrase with the foreign language.

1. Salut. Je m'appelle (your name).
Sah-loo. Zhuh mah-pell (your name).

2. Hola. Me llamo (your name).
OH-lah. May YAH-moh (your name).

Japanese   German   French

3. Aloha 'O-(your name), ko'u inoa.
Ah-LOH-hah OH-(your name), KOH-oo EE-noh-ah. ....

4. Ciao. Mi chiamo (your name).
Chow. MEE kee-AH-moh (your name). ....

5. Konnichiwa. (Your name) to iimasu.
**Kohn-nee-chee-wah. (Your name) toh
ee-mah-soo.**

....

6. Hallo. Ich heiße (your name).
HAHL-loh. Eehk HIGH-seh (your name). ....

Spanish   Italian   Hawaiian

Afternoon Snacks

Can you unscramble these special treats
that come from other countries?

Mexico
coats   tacos

England
ate dan nocess

Italy
zipaz

France
pecers

Germany
strezelp

Switzerland
tacoolech

Japan
uhiss

China
geg lorl

Hometown Cookin'

Complete each menu item with the name of the correct U.S. city listed below.

(Hint: The cities are well known for these foods.)

_ _ _ _ _ _ baked beans

_ _ _ _ _ _ _ chicken wings

_ _ _ _ _ _ _ _ _ _ _ _ sourdough bread

_ _ _ _ _ _ _ _ _ _ _ _ cheesesteak

_ _ _ _ _ _ _ _ _ _ jambalaya

_ _ _ _ _ _ _ deep-dish pizza

_ _ _ _ _ _ _ _ _ crab cakes

_ _ _ _ _ _ _ cheesecake

New York

Buffalo

Philadelphia

New Orleans

Boston

San Francisco

Baltimore

Chicago

Rise 'n' Shine

These are **real towns** in America! Can you match these silly towns with the states they call home?

You can get a nice cup of java at this town in Mississippi.

___ ___ _____

It's never lumpy in this town in Texas.

_____

Folks love this on their shortcakes in this California city.

_____

They make them sunny-side up or over easy in this town in Florida.

___ ___

With a little lettuce and tomato, this small town in Texas
is what sandwiches are made of.

_____

TODaY'S
SPECiaL:
TWO EGG, OaTMEAL,
BaCON, HOT COFFEE,
STRaWBERRY

Animal Alley

The animals are loose! Help them find their way back
to the real U.S. towns named in their honor.

WELCOME TO
DOGHOUSE
JUNCTION, CA

WELCOME TO
MONKEY'S
EYEBROW, KY

WELCOME TO
HUNGRY
HORSE, MT

WELCOME TO
ELEPHANT
BUTTE, NM

WELCOME TO
CAT ELBOW
CORNER, NY

WELCOME TO
MOSQUITO-
VILLE, VT

The Big What?

Can you match these cities with their famous nicknames?

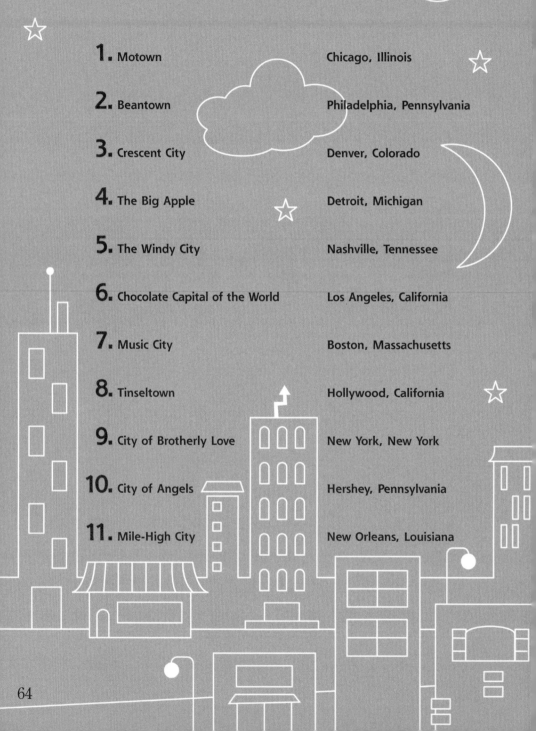

1. Motown   Chicago, Illinois

2. Beantown   Philadelphia, Pennsylvania

3. Crescent City   Denver, Colorado

4. The Big Apple   Detroit, Michigan

5. The Windy City   Nashville, Tennessee

6. Chocolate Capital of the World   Los Angeles, California

7. Music City   Boston, Massachusetts

8. Tinseltown   Hollywood, California

9. City of Brotherly Love   New York, New York

10. City of Angels   Hershey, Pennsylvania

11. Mile-High City   New Orleans, Louisiana

Lost at Sea

New shipmate buddies Nicole, Becky, Amanda, and Kayla are all staying on different decks on their cruise ship. But they can't remember where their rooms are! Can you **help them find their way** back to their rooms?

Remember, all four girls are staying on different decks.

The Adriatic has rooms numbered 100–299

The Caribbean Deck has rooms numbered 200–399.

The Caspian Deck has rooms numbered 300–499.

The Mediterranean Deck has rooms numbered 400–599.

Nicole remembers her room number was 455.

Kayla's room number started with a 4 too, but it definitely wasn't on a deck beginning with the letter C.

Becky's room was on a deck beginning with a C, but which one?

MEDITERRANEAN DECK >
< ADRIATIC DECK

Use this space to figure it out!

	Caribbean	Mediter-ranean	Caspian	Adriatic
Nicole				
Becky				
Amanda				
Kayla				

Vacation Vocab

Some of the best things about vacation can be found by searching up, down, backward, forward, and diagonally.

Adventure	Hike	Restaurant
Airplane	Holiday	Rides
Amusement Park	Hotel	Sand Castle
Beach	Laughs	Ski
Campground	Museum	Songs
Family	Picnic	Souvenir
Fun	Play	Swim
Games	Postcard	Surprises
	Relax	

```
W E U J M T O Z B Z L Z L P M
C R S U R P R I S E S B O Y u
A U Y R I N E V U O S S L A S
M T A O D O H L F R T I K D E
P N L L E Q E C E C M A V I u
G E P T S T K S A A X A A L M
R V Y X O L T R F E K I D O N
O D G H K A D D T H B R K H V
u A A M U S E M E N T P A R K
N O D R L A U G H S S L D F A
D H A R E L A X H G E A X A S
J N C I N C I P J R M N G O M
T E K I H F U N X A A E N I A
E L T S A C D N A S G G W u Y
J B T J O F F D X K S S I G O
```

Aquarium Encounters

Get ready for your visit to **the biggest aquarium in the world** by placing these freshwater and saltwater plants and creatures in the cross grid.

Hint: Start with the longest or the shortest word.

3 letters
Cod
Ray

4 Letters
Carp
Clam
Crab
Kelp
Reef

5 Letters
Coral
Perch
Trout
Whale

6 Letters
Shrimp
Walrus

7 Letters
Anemone
Dolphin
Man-o'-war
Octopus
Penguin
Piranha
Sea lion

8 Letters
Rockfish
Sailfish
Sea horse
Seashell
Starfish

9 Letters
Jellyfish

10 Letters
Whale shark
River otter

11 Letters
Electric eel

Zoo-ology

You have only a couple of hours to scope out the animals at the zoo. How many of these animals can you "find" in the cross grid?

3 Letters
Gnu

4 Letters
Lion

5 Letters
Camel
Koala
Tiger
Zebra

6 Letters
Jaguar
Python

7 Letters
Cheetah
Gazelle
Giraffe
Gorilla
Leopard

8 Letters
Antelope
Elephant

9 Letters
Alligator
Polar Bear

10 Letters
Giant Panda

11 Letters
Rattlesnake

12 Letters
Hippopotamus

14 Letters
Tasmanian Devil

Detour

There's a detour on the way to your ski resort. Find your way through this maze if you want to hit the slopes before dinner.

Start

Finish

Travel Secrets

Can you crack the code to decipher these travel tips? We've filled in a few letters to give you a head start.

1.

$\frac{S}{21}\frac{}{3}\frac{}{1}\quad \frac{}{5}\frac{}{10}\frac{E}{7}\frac{E}{7}\frac{S}{21}\frac{E}{7}!\quad \frac{}{6}\frac{}{17}\frac{}{16}\text{’}\frac{T}{22}\quad \frac{}{8}\frac{}{17}\frac{}{20}\frac{}{9}\frac{E}{7}\frac{T}{22}$

$\frac{}{1}\frac{}{17}\frac{}{23}\frac{}{20}\quad \frac{}{5}\frac{}{3}\frac{M}{15}\frac{E}{7}\frac{}{20}\frac{}{3}\quad \frac{}{3}\frac{}{16}\frac{}{6}\quad \frac{}{8}\frac{}{11}\frac{}{14}\frac{M}{15}.$

2.

$\frac{}{8}\frac{}{11}\frac{}{14}\frac{}{14}\quad \frac{}{3}\quad \frac{B}{4}\frac{}{3}\frac{}{5}\frac{}{13}\frac{}{18}\frac{}{3}\frac{}{5}\frac{}{13}\quad \frac{}{25}\frac{}{11}\frac{}{22}\frac{}{10}$

$\frac{B}{4}\frac{}{3}\frac{}{5}\frac{}{13}\quad \frac{S}{21}\frac{E}{7}\frac{}{3}\frac{T}{22}\quad \frac{B}{4}\frac{}{17}\frac{}{20}\frac{E}{7}\quad \frac{}{6}\frac{}{17}\frac{}{15}\quad \frac{B}{4}\frac{M}{23}\frac{S}{21}\frac{}{22}\quad \frac{E}{7}\frac{}{20}\frac{S}{21}.$

3.

$\frac{}{10}\frac{}{3}\frac{}{24}\frac{E}{7}\quad \frac{E}{7}\frac{}{26}\frac{}{5}\frac{}{11}\frac{T}{22}\frac{}{11}\frac{}{16}\frac{}{9}\quad \frac{}{3}\frac{}{6}\frac{}{24}\frac{E}{7}\frac{}{16}\frac{T}{22}\frac{}{23}\frac{}{20}\frac{E}{7}\frac{S}{21}!$

4.

$\frac{}{18}\frac{}{3}\frac{}{5}\frac{}{13}\quad \frac{}{3}\quad \frac{S}{21}\frac{}{15}\frac{}{11}\frac{}{14}\frac{E}{7}\quad \frac{}{3}\frac{}{16}\frac{}{6}\quad \frac{}{10}\frac{}{3}\frac{}{24}\frac{E}{7}\quad \frac{}{3}$

$\frac{}{8}\frac{}{3}\frac{B}{4}\frac{}{23}\frac{}{14}\frac{}{17}\frac{}{23}\frac{S}{21}\quad \frac{T}{22}\frac{}{11}\frac{M}{15}\frac{E}{7}!$

Airport Adventures

Nicole and her family got to the airport just in time for their flight to Florida. But they may have missed a few things in their race to the gate. Can you spot the five problems in this picture?

List the problems:

1.

2.

3.

4.

5.

Answers

Vanity Tags (page 54)

1. Creative, 2. I Skate (or Ice Skate), 3. Aye, Aye, Captain,
4. Doll Lover, 5. Love to Swim, 6. Pizza Lover, 7. Just Because
8. Ready to Ski, 9. Late for Class, 10. Howdy Do (or How Do You Do),
11. Tennis, Anyone, 12. Super Family, 13. G'day, Mate, 14. Awesome
Trip, 15. I'll Be Seeing You, 16. Two and Two Are Four, 17. Animal Lover

Highway Puzzlers (page 55)

1. Railroad Crossing, 2. Slippery When Wet, 3. Camping, 4. Picnic Area,
5. Keep Left, 6. Moose Crossing, 7. Library, 8. No Parking,
9. Alligator Crossing, 10. Playground, 11. Bicycle Route,
12. Hospital, 13. Construction Ahead, 14. Winding Road

Baggage Claim (page 56)

Souvenirs for Sale (page 57)

Amount Spent

				Money Left Over
David	2.20	5.00	7.00	.80
Emily	12.50	1.00	.50	1.00
Alexis	2.20	12.00	.50	.30
Matt	2.20	1.00	1.00	10.80

Matt's the only one with enough money left, and he treats his sisters to two scoops. Then they all pool their change, so David can have a cone, too.

Making Friends All Over the World (pages 58–59)

1. French, 2. Spanish, 3. Hawaiian, 4. Italian,
5. Japanese, 6. German

Afternoon Snacks (page 60)

tacos, tea and scones, pizza, crepes, pretzels,
chocolate, sushi, egg roll

Hometown Cookin' (page 61)

Boston, Buffalo, San Francisco, Philadelphia,
New Orleans, Chicago,
Baltimore, New York

Rise 'n' Shine (page 62)

Hot Coffee, MS; Oatmeal, TX; Strawberry, CA;
Two Egg, FL; Bacon, TX

The Big What? (page 64)

1. Detroit, MI, 2. Boston, MA, 3. New Orleans, LA, 4. New York, NY,
5. Chicago, IL, 6. Hershey, PA, 7. Nashville, TN, 8. Hollywood, CA,
9. Philadelphia, PA, 10. Los Angeles, CA, 11. Denver, CO

Lost at Sea (page 65)

Nicole—Caspian; Becky—Caribbean; Amanda—Adriatic; Kayla—Mediterranean

Vacation Vocab (pages 66–67)

Animal Alley (page 63)

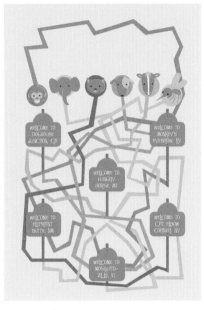

W E U J M T O Z B Z L Z L P M
C R S U R P R I S E S B O Y u
A U Y R I N E V U O S S L A S
M T A O D O H L F R T I K D E
P N L L E Q E C E C M A V I u
G E P T S T K S A A X A A L M
R V Y X O L T R F E K I D O N
O D G H K A D D T H B R K H V
u A A M U S E M E N T P A R K
N O D R L A U G H S S L D F A
D H A R E L A X H G E A X A S
J N C I N C I P J R M N G O M
T E K I H F U N X A A E N I A
E L T S A C D N A S G G W u Y
J B T J O F F D X K S S I G O

77

Aquarium Encounters (pages 68–69)

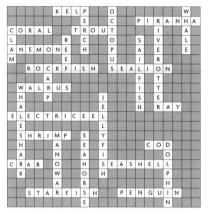

Zoo-ology (pages 70–71)

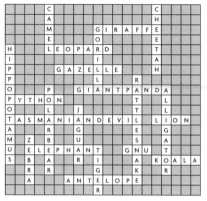

Detour (page 72)

Travel Secrets (page 73)

A-3	J-12	S-21
B-4	K-13	T-22
C-5	L-14	U-23
D-6	M-15	V-24
E-7	N-16	W-25
F-8	O-17	X-26
G-9	P-18	Y-1
H-10	Q-19	Z-2
I-11	R-20	

1. Say cheese! Don't forget your camera and film.
2. Fill a backpack with backseat boredom busters.
3. Have exciting adventures!
4. Pack a smile and have a fabulous time!

Airport Adventures (page 74)

Dad's still in his pajamas, Mom has two different shoes on, and little brother put his underpants on over his clothes! Nicole's teddy bear is falling out of her backpack, and they are at the wrong gate!

Drop us a vacation postcard!

Mail to:
Travel Editor
American Girl
8400 Fairway Place
Middleton, WI 53562

Here are some other American Girl books you might like:

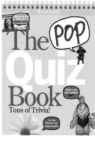

❑ I read it.

❑ I read it.

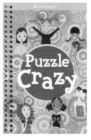

❑ I read it.

❑ I read it.

❑ I read it.

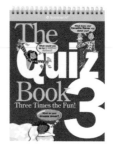

❑ I read it.

❑ I read it.

❑ I read it.

❑ I read it.

Story Starters

Use one of the story starters below, and take turns adding sentences to the story.

1. When the (your family name here) **family bought their tickets to the traveling circus, they had no idea . . .**

2. (Your name here) **bravely climbed into the front-row seat of the roller coaster, and then suddenly . . .**

3. The (your family name here) **family opened the hotel room door, ready to begin their sightseeing adventure. But they weren't expecting . . .**

4. Everybody said the old hotel was haunted, but the (your family name here) **family didn't believe them until the clock chimed midnight and . . .**

Road Trip

Everyone in the car takes part in this game to see if you can reach the number one hundred without making a mistake.

- Take turns counting, beginning with number one.

- Every time you get to a number that's a multiple of three (3, 6, 9), say **"road"** instead of the number.

- When you reach a multiple of five (5, 10, 15), say **"trip"** instead of the number.

- When you reach a multiple of both (15, 30, 45), say **"road trip!"**

- If you forget to say "road" or "trip," you have to start over. How far can you go before your road trip runs off course?

Alphabet Name Game

Here's a twist on an alphabet name game you've probably played before. Take turns singing or chanting for each letter of the alphabet.

A, my name is Annie and I'm **going** to Alabama. I'm going to **bring** my automobile and **drive** it to the aquarium.

B, my name is Barbara and I'm going to Boston. I'm going to bring my ball and bounce it in the ball field.

C, my name is Connie and I'm going to California. I'm going to bring my camera and take pictures at the campground.

Backseat Song

Make the time go faster by adding new words to old favorites! See who can come up with the funniest lyrics.

Here's one to sing to the tune of "99 Bottles of Pop on the Wall":

100 exits to go on the road,
100 exits to go.
If one of those exits should happen to pass,
99 exits to go on the road.
99 exits to go on the road,
99 exits to go . . .

Cloud Cartoons

This is a great game to play when there are big fluffy clouds in the sky.

Lean back (everyone except the driver, that is) and look up into the sky.

What kinds of pictures can you find in the clouds? A bunny rabbit? A birthday cake? A wizard with a long beard?

Do you all see the same shapes, or can you find different pictures in the clouds?

License Plate Puzzle

Make up crazy sentences to match the letters of the license plates you see.

KMJ =
Kittens Must Jump

BXA =
Bicycle X-rays Aardvark

AZY =
All Zebras Yodel

Royal Speech

Talk to each other like princes and princesses for the next ten minutes. Here are some examples to get you started:

Speaker one: "My ladies, there's a fast food eating establishment ahead. Shall we stop for an afternoon repast?"

Speaker two: "Oh yes, Prince Fancypants. I'd be delighted to dine on some royal road food."

Speaker three: "Please remind the servant that we will require a royal strawberry shake."

Speaker four: "Remember to take only the most delicate of sips through your straw."

Story Starters

Use one of the story starters below, and take turns adding sentences to the story.

1. Obviously, it was a case of mistaken identity when the strange woman tried to hand (your name here) a bag of money . . .

2. One trail went right, the other veered left. (Your name here) took a deep breath and . . .

3. The boy sitting on the bench at the amusement park turned to (your name here) and said, "You can't tell a soul . . ."

4. "You have just won a one-hour shopping spree," the store manager told (your name here). "There's just one catch . . ."

Cow Counter

Play this game one-on-one, or form teams.

First, decide on the place or time (like the state line or lunchtime) where you'll stop counting. Then count the cows on your side of the road while the other player(s) count cows on the other side.

No cows on your route? Choose another thing to count, like red cars, Volkswagen bugs, or motorcycles.

Packing Your Suitcase

Players take turns "packing" a suitcase, coming up with items from A to Z.

Player one might say, "I am going on a trip and in my suitcase is an apron . . ."

Player two would add, "I am going on a trip and in my suitcase is an apron and a bathing suit . . ."

Player three (or player one if there are only two of you) would add a "C" word, like coat or clogs.

Pack your bags from A to Z!

Backseat Song

Write your own lyrics to the tune of "Twinkle, Twinkle, Little Star":

Driving, driving on the road,
Our trunk is full of a heavy load:
My sister's skis and my brother's weights.
Did Mom forget my new ice skates?
We have everything, Dad hopes.
Tomorrow morning we hit the slopes!

Guess What?

Choose someone to be "It." That person announces that he or she is a person, a place, or a thing. Then the rest of you ask questions like, "Are you blue?" or "Do you taste good?" or "Do you have four legs?" until you guess the right answer. The person who guesses right gets to be "It" next, or, if your family likes to be equitable, take turns being "It."

"ARE YOU
AN ELF?"
"YES!"

License-Plate Word Find

Create as many words as you can from the letters in license plates. You can add more letters, but all three letters must be included in your words.

CTF =
terrific, fantastic

YLP =
play, yelp, loopy

GTI =
night, tiger, gift

Astronaut-ese

Talk to each other in "astronautical" style ONLY for the next ten minutes.

Here are some examples to get you started:

Speaker one: "Houston, the time is 0500 hours. How much longer before we land on Mars?"

Speaker two: "By my calculations, at five times the speed of sound, we should enter Mars's orbit in precisely 35 minutes."

Speaker three: "Flight captain, I detect space junk ahead. We might have to detour through the Andromeda Galaxy."

Speaker four: "Hold on! I'm going to launch us into warp speed!"

Story Starters

Use one of the story starters below, and take turns adding sentences to the story.

1. (Your name here) smoothed out the old map. "Can this place really exist?"

2. The sun was setting as the first of the vampire bats took flight, and (your name here) was all alone in the middle of the desert.

3. The wind howled and clouds opened up. (Your name here) bravely clung to the small raft as the waves pushed her farther and farther away from shore.

4. At the (your family name here) family reunion, no one could believe it when (relative's name here) arrived and . . .

Billboard Alphabet

Starting with A, find words on signs that begin with each letter of the alphabet (you can decide ahead of time to skip Q, X, and Z if all the players agree).

Read billboards, road signs, bumper stickers, and even ads on the sides of trucks to "travel" from A to Z.

Turn it into a race!

Form teams of front seat versus backseat, right side of the car versus left side, or boys against girls.

APPLES $1.25
BANANAS $2
CARROTS $1.50

Song Stumper
Test your musical smarts.

Hum the first few bars of a popular song. How quickly can the others in the car guess the name of the tune? The first person to guess correctly tries to stump you with a song next.

HUM HUM HMM
HMMM HAHUMM
HUUUM HUMM
HMMMMMMMMMM
HMMM HUM HUM HMM
HMMM HAHUMM
HOOOM HOUUUHM
HUUUUMMMMMM HOM
HUM HUM HUM
HUMMM MMM...

Spy Talk

Talk to each other like international spies for the next ten minutes.

Here are some examples to get you started:

Speaker one: "Don't blow our cover. The people in the next car think we're an average family, not an international spy ring."

Speaker two: "But the bad guys are gaining on us. If we don't reach our secret headquarters soon, the world as we know it will end."

Speaker three: "Don't listen to him! He's a double agent. We must push on to save the world."

Speaker four: "But first we have to stop at the rest area. It's time to refuel our electro spy mobile."

Story Starters

Use one of the story starters below, and take turns adding sentences to the story.

1. Who would've thought anything exciting could happen at a rest area, but when the (your family name here) family stopped for a break, they saw . . .

2. When their car ran out of gas in the middle of the Arizona desert highway, the (your family name here) family never thought they'd be rescued by . . .

3. The (your name here) family loved the dude ranch until the chuck wagon pulled up and . . .

4. It was starting to get dark and Dad had just suggested we stop for dinner when (your name here) spotted the strange object hovering in the sky . . .

Loony Landscape

If the view out the window is boring, invent your own scene.

You'll need pens and paper to play. To start, draw a face. The next player adds something, like a body or hair. Take turns adding to the drawing. Add anything you can think of—the sillier the better! The game ends when nothing else can be squeezed into the drawing.

Create Your Own Rainbow

Have a race to see who can be the first to spot six cars in the colors of the rainbow.

Make the game even more exciting by finding the colors in order, forward and then backward. Give yourself bonus points for spotting black and white cars on either end of the rainbow. A rare gold car at the end of the rainbow makes you the grand prize winner! You get to choose the next game.

Are you in the airport or on a train? Have a race to see who can be the first to spot travelers wearing the colors of the rainbow.

Story Starters

Use one of the story starters below, and take turns adding sentences to the story.

1. When the famous movie star saw the (your family name here) family waiting in line for his autograph, he . . .

2. It was a lovely flower-strewn meadow, and the (your family name here) family didn't think twice about gathering a bouquet until . . .

3. When the (your family name here) family visited the White House, they lost their tour guide and . . .

4. It was a dark and stormy night. Suddenly, the (your family name here) family's campfire . . .

Silent Signals

Play this game when the driver tells you to be quiet!

To start, lean forward so that the other player can reach your back. She thinks of a word, then writes it on your back with her finger, spelling it one letter at a time. If you don't understand a letter, ask for a repeat by flapping your arms like a chicken. When the word has been written out, whisper what you think it was.

Note: If you can't play this way while keeping your seatbelt safely buckled, try writing on each other's forearms.

If you're wrong, the other player spells it out again. If you're right, trade places and play again.

Hide-and-Squeak

Try this car-sized version of an old favorite.

To start, think of a specific place in the car where a mouse could hide, such as in a cup under the driver's seat, under a map in the glove compartment, or in Mom's purse. Write it down and keep it out of sight. The other player has to guess where to find the mouse. Respond to each guess by squeaking loudly if the guess was close to the hiding place or squeaking quietly if it was far away. Keep playing until the mouse is found.

SQUEAK! SQUEAK!

You will need:

Two or more players, a game piece for each player (a button, a coin, or any small object will do), and dice (from the back of the book).

THERE

Punch out these dice, fold along the scored lines, and slip the tab in place to keep closed.

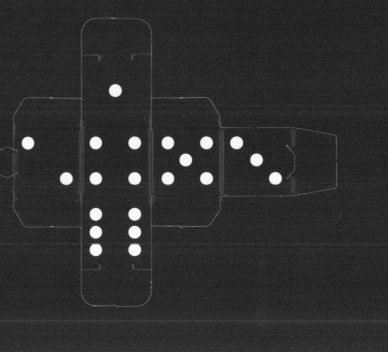